AF632660

Mediator

Sydney Aguas

BookLeaf Publishing

Mediator © 2023 Sydney Aguas

All rights reserved.

No part of this publication may be reproduced, stored in a retrieval system, or transmitted, in any form or by any means, electronic, mechanical, photocopying, recording or otherwise, without the prior written permission of the presenters.

Sydney Aguas asserts the moral right to be identified as author of this work.

Presentation by *BookLeaf Publishing*

Web: www.bookleafpub.com

E-mail: info@bookleafpub.com

ISBN: 9789357213073

First edition 2023

Atonement (Romans 5:7-8)

Guilty head on the block.
The axe of justice falls--snap!
The innocent head rolls.

Unclean (Isaiah 5:1-6)

I stand in the midst of glory, gold;
Surpassing, subsuming, suffocating.
The incense of divinity sweeps into my nostrils,
Thick smoke burning my lungs--
I cannot stand, in the midst of glory.

I stand in the presence of holy, white;
Slicing, scathing, searing.
The fires of purity seep into my mouth,
Flames blistering my lips and tongue--
I cannot stand, in the presence of the holy.

Is it the hiss of angels' wings or my own
thoughts whispering?
The weight of glory will consume me;
The force of holiness undo me;
"I am unclean, unclean, unclean!"

Yet, your spirit fills my nostrils, my mouth, my
lungs;
It slips past my lips and sparks on my tongue--
Until I hear you whispering,
"Your guilt is paid. Take my hand."
--And I can stand.
I understand:
I am clean, I am clean, I am clean!

Consuming Fire (Hebrews 12:28-29)

I was taught terror
In the shadow of cathedral spires
Under the glowering gaze of immortal saints
Of the judgement impending
Wrath--bright, brazen, burning
Reserved for the doubting, debauched, depraved
Destined for a lake that flames
Body, mind, and soul--in the end, consumed.

I was shown truth
In the light of sacred words
From the wondrous words of a gentle, ancient voice
Of forgiveness unending
Love--bold, brilliant, blazing
Offered to the hurting, hungry, hopeless
Pursued with a devotion that flames
Body, mind, and soul--in the end, consumed.

Healing (Hosea 6:1-2)

A surgeon wounds in order to save;
Wound and save me.

Relief cannot come before the pain;
Give pain and relief to me.

What isn't broken cannot mend;
Break and mend me.

Before you heal, you must hurt--
So hurt and heal me.

Beauty for Ashes (Isaiah 61:1-3)

What has been broken can be bound.
What has been taken can be found.

What has been tainted can be made pure.
What has been used can be restored.

What has been lost can be retrieved.
What has been ruined can be redeemed.

For our hurts, he will give us healing.
For our sorrows, he gives us singing.

For our mistakes, he gives us grace.
For our fears, he will give us peace.

For our hearts, he gives us eternity.
For our ashes, he will give us beauty.

Unto Us (Isaiah 9:6)

On a world that slept in darkness, there once broke a splendid light.
It was as if the sum of heaven's stars had chosen to descend--
On a world suspended in darkness, waiting for a glimpse of the divine.
So when this light, like a beacon, illuminated the way for those who were lost--
In darkness, we found no better word for it's brilliance than "miracle".
This miracle came first to a young couple, in the form of a son.

The young man and his wife knew their child was not common; their son--
Seemed, even from birth, to be filled with that wondrous light.
They watched the light shine as he grew, cherishing him as their miracle.
Yet, he was not proud, but chose with humility to descend,
And befriend, the lowest in the world: the outcast, oppressed, and lost.
He loved us, and we followed him; he told us of things eternal and divine.

Some of us believed his words, and even trusted that he was divine;
Others, with spite, said that he was nothing more than a carpenter's son.
They rejected the love and truth he shared, and remained lost.
Writhing, they recoiled when he dispelled their darkness with light.
Rather than being lifted up, they preferred to descend--
Further into blindness, despising the miracle.

Despising no one, he offered all the hope of a miracle.
In his words we found healing, peace, and love divine.
We knew he would not allow us to descend,
But raise us up, helping us as a father helps his son.
Wherever he went, lives were changed as they stepped into the light.
We wept for joy, knowing we were not forever lost.

For a while, those who hated him worried all was lost,
Until they devised a plot to obliterate the miracle.

The spreading shadow threatened to snuff out the light.
Mankind brought death to the divine--
By crucifying a carpenter's son.
Into the darkness of a tomb, they watched his body descend.

For three journeys of the sun, we saw all our hopes descend.
The world, again, plunged in silent darkness, utterly lost.
We watched and waited: every father, mother, daughter, and son.
Then, we trembled with fear and joy, witnessing history's greatest miracle.
We would pass down how we saw death defeated by the divine,
Dazzling the darkness, filling every shadowed, broken place with iridescent light.

Unto us a son, for love, chose to descend,
Like a shining light, to our world, dark and lost;
A miracle unrivaled, our own glimpse of the divine.

Heirs (Romans 8:16-17)

Once I was a child,
A nameless wanderer, lost and alone, without an identity;
Now I have a name.

Once I was an orphan,
A fatherless seeker, searching for a place to call home;
Now I have a Father.

Once I was a bastard,
A futureless offspring left without the hope of an inheritance;
Now I have a future.

Now I am an heir.

Incorruptible (1 Corinthians 15:51-53)

The flower in winter's first frost;
It's delicate beauty withering in the bitter cold--
Everything fades.

The last light of day;
The final bright beams blinking out before the dark--
Everything ends.

The face of an aging loved one;
Their familiar features shriveling with the touch of time--
Everything dies.

But not I.

As a butterfly,
Hidden for a time only to break through, transformed;
I will change.

As a seedling,
Buried in the earth for a time only to burst forth, reborn;
I will resurrect.

As a bird--
Falls to the ground for a time only to catch the wind, and soars;
I will rise--

Incorruptible.

Pearl of Price (Matthew 13:45-46)

I searched the earth to find a treasure rare,
A costly gift that no one else had found,
The thing to which no other could compare,
More precious than the gems beneath the ground.

Then I found the prize that I keenly sought;
The treasure that transcends my heart's desires.
This is a gift that must be dearly bought.
Yet, I will give whatever it requires.

Few know the worth of what I have obtained;
It's greater than all other wealth to me.
But it is hidden and not easily gained,
Like a shining pearl deep in the sea.

Though I know the cost I paid is steep,
This pearl of highest price is mine to keep.

Religion (Romans 3)

Where is goodness in the human heart?
Can one find purity that isn't flawed?
Few men will strive some kindness to impart,
While many will by evil whims be drawn.

Those who wish to combat this wicked root--
Aim to achieve a series of good deeds.
Many find religion in this pursuit--
Will offer the morality they need.

But the piety of such things rings false--
When to temptations holy ones succumb.
In the reality of human fault,
The one who hopes for righteousness turns numb.

Religion cannot cleanse our inward filth,
And no good deed will the human soul save.
It is faith that reveals a higher truth,
And grace that keeps us from the gaping grave.

Faith that we are forgiven every sin;
Grace to accept that all our debts are paid--
By one who loved the human soul within,
Enough to give his life for ours instead.

Mediator (1 Timothy 2:5-6)

He knew the realms of glory bathed in breathtaking light.
He knew the surpassing power of divine might.
He knew the unending chorus that the angels sang above.
He knew the soul-shattering beauty of his Father's love.

Then, for one pivotal moment, as the universe paused in its course,
At the word of his Father, he came descended from heaven to us…

And he knew the hunger and cold we feel on hopeless nights.
He knew the lure of temptation for something in his sight.
He knew sorrow and rejection so deep it took his breath,
And when he was abandoned, he met the sting of death.

When divinity embraced humanity, our world would never be the same.

The son of God took on humanity so he could embrace our pain.

Jesus transcended the ancient divide between mortal and divine.
When he became our mediator, the hearts of God and man aligned.

First Love (1 John 4:10)

Before I knew your name,
You fixed your heart on my soul.
Before I ever saw your face,
You promised to make me whole.

With love fierce and tender,
You vowed to hold my life,
To be helper and defender,
My deliverer from strife.

You were not my first desire.
Yet, you did not think twice.
Whatever price was required,
You would make the sacrifice.

At first, I shunned you foolishly;
I was bitter, blind and lost.
To redeem me and set me free,
You paid a steep and fatal cost.

Your face is dear to me now.
I rejoice to hear your name.
You loved me first to show me how--
To love others just the same.

Evidence Unseen (Hebrews 11:1)

That which hovers in between--
The spirit and the carnal plane--
Is evidence of the unseen.

My sight may fail to explain--
What I resolutely believe;
Yet it's substance will remain.

Consider, how we can't perceive--
The gentle brush of wind we feel,
As it whispers through the leaves.

My senses cannot reveal--
The strength of love and forgiveness;
Yet, their power is no less real.

I proceed in persistence,
Though the doubtful disagree,
Futile in their resistance.

Faith trusts the truth of what will be;
So I choose to be confident--
Of hopes that I have yet to see.

Good & Perfect Things
(James 1:17)

When, in the morning, our eyes open,
Pulling back their drowsy hoods,
All our senses are invited--
To witness something good:

The afternoon light glinting gold in strands of hair;
The bewitching sound of music drifting on the air;

The comfort of homecoming, after many days away;
The joy of meeting with dear friends, which words cannot convey.

And if, in life, we strive--
To keep our eyes open and reflect,
We will, in a moment,
Witness something perfect:

The sound of happy laughter ringing through your home;
The eager touch of your lover's lips as they meet your own;

The bit of heaven that you glimpse in your
newborn's eyes;
The whisper of forgiveness just before your
parent dies.

Yet, all these things do not exceed--
The source from which they spring.
It is the love of God that grants--
All good and perfect things.

Earthen Vessels (2 Corinthians 4:7)

We were never meant to be--
Shining works of majesty,
Glittering for all to see;
Stars blazing in the night.

We aren't made to draw the eye,
To take the wings of pride, and fly,
To raise ourselves up ever high;
Gold sunbeams burning bright.

We may not be grand or bold.
Our value is in what we hold,
Glistening like bits of gold,
Hidden gems of light.

We are vessels made of earth,
Humble from our time of birth;
We keep a truth of wondrous worth,
The source of our delight.

Senseless Peace (Philippians 4:6-7)

When trials threaten to undo me,
A furious storm that does not cease.
I sense it running through me:
An overwhelming peace.

When fears creep in and torture me,
Choking vines that don't release.
It breaks the bonds and frees me,
This all-consuming peace.

When sorrow overcomes me,
Powerful waves that only increase,
I feel it filling and lifting me,
This undergirding peace.

Though it is not clear to me
Why my hope has not deceased,
I know it will sustain me,
This strong but senseless peace.

The Weight of Glory (2 Corinthians 4:17)

No matter how heavy our troubles become,
Though they bear down on us endlessly,
They do not outweigh the glory to come.

With courage, we strengthen our hearts,
Willing them to beat on faithfully--
No matter how heavy our troubles become.

When trials, like clouds, do not depart,
There is a light that we still see:
They do not outweigh the glory to come

Though we almost give way, crumbling apart,
We do not break entirely--
No matter how heavy our troubles become

When this life ends, a new life will start;
Our present pains will be a memory.
They do not outweigh the glory to come.

We cling to this hope with every part:
Our sorrows will not last eternally.
No matter how heavy our troubles become,
They do not outweigh the glory to come.

Conquerors (2 Corinthians 4:8-9)

Bruised but not beaten;
Oppressed but not overtaken.
Though woes leave our hearts sore,
We shall triumph in this war.

Stricken but not stranded;
Abused but not abandoned.
Divine love thrives at our core.
We have hope for what's in store.

Mistreated but not forsaken;
Persecuted but not shaken.
We rise more victorious than before,
Conquerors all, and so much more…

Deep to Deep (Psalm 42:7)

A million voices call out to me;
A cacophony of birdsong and fluttering wings,
Or the screaming of wind in the midst of a
storm.

But your voice is the whisper of a winding
stream;
Gently running over the surface of my mind,
Clearing away worries that clouded its clarity.

Your voice is in the rumble of a rushing river;
Flowing through the caverns of my heart,
Stirring up truths that long sat still.

Your voice is in the mighty roar of waterfalls;
Cascading down to the depths of my soul,
Bursting upon it with a flood of joy.

Your voice is the rhythm of the tides;
Pulsing deeply in the core of my spirit,
Drowning me in wave upon wave of love.

Known (Psalm 139:1-18)

It is as a man and his wife:
Their hearts are two vines from the same root--
Twisting, intertwining, always bound.
Their bodies are familiar ground,
Etched with well-worn paths that lead home…

But no--
Their love is not potent enough.
Their bond is not strong enough.

It is as a mother and her child:
Their hearts are the moon and sun--
One reflecting the other's pure light;
Their bodies are a tree with branches wide,
Extensions of one another that ever grow…

But no--
Their unity does not go far enough.
Their understanding does not run deep enough.

I am infinitely more to you;
We are united through and through,
With an understanding clear and true,
And a bond that is unbreakable;
A love that's inescapable

You are infinitely more to me;
You are with me, and through me, and in me;
You see who I was, who I am, and will be;
Perfectly, eternally--
You know me.

Beloved (Jeremiah 31:3)

Oh Beloved mine, you are most beautiful to me.
You beam with light, your eyes shine as the sea.
There is only perfection in every part of you.
There is no one on earth more faithful, more true;
You stand with me unwaveringly.

Without you, I dread where I would be.
Like a captive, I was bound until you set me free.
I was lost in darkness, with no one to lead me through;
Consumed with despair 'till you came to my rescue,
Oh Beloved mine.

Only you can know me so intimately--
And want me, despite all the flaws you see.
You've shown me a love that I never knew,
Oh Beloved mine.

Beyond this life, and into eternity,
Our precious love shall ever be.
No power on this earth can undo--
The covenant that binds we two;

For I will be yours eternally…
Oh Beloved mine.

www.ingramcontent.com/pod-product-compliance
Lightning Source LLC
Chambersburg PA
CBHW051758130826
49812CB00033B/1191
* 9 7 8 9 3 5 7 2 1 3 0 7 3 *